THE INSIDE OF AN APPLE

JOSHUA BECKMAN

The Inside of an Apple

WAVE BOOKS

SEATTLE AND

NEW YORK

Published by Wave Books www.wavepoetry.com

Wave Books titles are distributed to the trade by
Consortium Book Sales and Distribution
Phone: 800-283-3572 / SAN 631-760x

This title is available in limited edition hardcover
directly from the publisher

Library of Congress Cataloging-in-Publication Data
Beckman, Joshua, 1971–
The inside of an apple / Joshua Beckman. — First edition.
pages cm
ISBN 978-1-933517-78-0 (limited edition hardcover)
ISBN 978-1-933517-75-9 (trade paperback; alk. paper)
I. Title.
PS3552.E2839157 2013
811'.54—dc23
2012050222

Printed in the United States of America

The author wishes to thank his family and friends, as well as The
Brother in Elysium for publishing *POEMS* and *Porch Light (lamp
and chair)*, where some of the poems from this book first appeared.

9 8 7 6 5 4 3 2

Wave Books 037

*

THE INSIDE OF AN APPLE

Stars
that form from bells
    planes that act
like stars
        drunk blue
palette of early
night
            in which
an electric
light swings
over the yard
    it is a branch

I live
and on one mountain
then the next
the sun shines down

a batch of metal pole clanks
and makes a music sound
in the quiet
air sound sounds

on the lit hill trees
tall before a white cloud mountain
and seen

I saw them yesterday
and again today they're shown to me

bird & stream
on tree as we passed
the green
moss and tweet
this morning's
river fog was
flat bright there
like seeing things
apple branches empty
barely <u>bark frost scene</u>
river's graceful turning
not to be believed

<u>the inside</u>

<u>of an apple</u>

                                      burning fall
and wood making heat
also there are no stars
in the dark sky
                          grey
clouds bunch together
with closed down houses
      and dog bark wind

I saw a picture being still
and I was still too
having seen something.

I sit most days on the porch
and sometimes one might hear
the clock clock of my heels
getting lost and sometimes

everyone in town is gone to sleep
and I step out into the street
so I might see a thing
and see a thing I do.

Big grey street
and silver snow
and silver sky

These bars on tracks
as trains do ride

       empty field
covering the ground
with little bits of its stone
dipping down and
       sloping upward

so always where the earth is
no one's really there.

Along the river
in my canoe I rowed
while the plain pink sun
lit the snowy pines
ain't it pretty.
Water filling the lowlands
in a cold ramble
as if from the inside.
Up top big snowy graveyards
of exaggerated grace.
Like the world,
the love of my late life
was a moss,
bright as heaven's maybe home
it gets all puffed up teary
and when the sun comes out
it feels different different
different. I think I'm
describing a storm cloud
look how it acts
other than it was.

Quit &
unextinguished
      like stupid
  child's wooden box

a lamp
      a fire, a scroll
and a wastebasket made
from the body of a tree

In my chair I waited
while on some mountain
nearby there was
cold beautiful snow
I was certain.

Silver streamers dazzling winter

I let my body down slow which is
what they say to do, like a whale
with its breathing and floating
in the ocean.

Yesterday
was the half moon
and today was basically
the half moon too.

A glacier's blue
and water
in the middle of a lake
is blue.

I only had one day
during which I could get myself
out into the middle of it

and I did,

                kudos to me.

And to the resilient goose
  who never feels cold
And to the talky crow
  who has so many friends
And to the inspiring stealthy ducks
  who fly together in clips above water.

It's a silly betrayal
of my own thoughts
to invent or remember,
so maybe I'll just close
with these tender lines
of Henry David Thoreau:

"An oak tree
  in Hubbard's Passage
stands absolutely
  motionless
and dark
against the sky."

In the air along the river
sailed beauty and cuspish the swallow
sweet brown dirt caked in the banks
made us think, and the water
which surrounded our legs made us feel
and then the boat drifted back
into the hollow.

        Sympathy excited
   is the basis
        of remarkable love

and friendship, as was
classically described with
a kind of current everchanging
its form
  translates as
         object made of
      stone or clover

they're so strange with
their cut-off arms and noses

How vacant is the real unseeing stare,
they want to call it dead but dead's
too much alive.

Things made tart
      not to eat
      but to
    peel off
      with my teeth
and taste it
      then
     <u>as russet apples</u>
in some fall scene
      look dirty I guess
hanging from
     otherwise lovely trees
     and falling onto
the still green grass
    one last time
        piggish
  and round

I'm not with my blue toes or my doggies
nor am I under any arched roof rotting blossoms
in my drain, sunlight pouncing upon me,
nor am I fixed like a tree, nor am I unfixed
like a wind. I ate an apple, that's fine
and after Anthony left I got a whiskey.
I stared a bit like a shadow at a book,
a fold in my shirt showed a monk's bowing head
in a column of dusty light, but I just basically
used it to cover up my arm which was prickling
now because of some awful thing within me.
Big nasty sun making me feel old and then
this lovely gold bird flew up to my lunch.
An actual family of little white turnips
rolling over in the boiling pot like some
clouds is how I act. A great blue sky for a bed
and that beauty make me happy again.

That being alive
  the bees buzz round
not fields in which their lovely flowers grow
but a big plaster apartment
kinda honey and yellow

  light comes in at fantastical angles
alive and sweet
    like the human people with their food

It's a magical thing I felt
  compounding its spark within me
 as those pulsing sounds began to speak
      saying, you're so gone you'll never come back

  and then from out of my ass
  fell that little ball of wax

silvered out night
abstract as a bath
and cloudy as a little cup
of white tea
or a window
or a streetlamp

(later)

it's rainy
and the cool air
is all around my head

*

flecks
of another
fleeing naked ass
in apartment

(cold rose soap)

I'm naked too
and sick

a kind of
blood song
falls out of me

(aug 27 or 8)

damp sprung run
of dirty clothes
    play on my bed
and lamplight
    (August 28)
      summer's alaska
crooked on the wall
    and clapping of dishes
in the woo woo kitchen
      puts me to sleep
chilly or no

rain stones curved
   and washed right down
the cold water's
    big white sound
   wrapped in cloth
    in cloth foresending
I leave my bed
   and there you are
where the shirt's balled up
   in the lawn by the poppies

flowers from
the outside
now, full of
living water
like a cloud

stations formed and made
　　　　on beachy sands
　　and waiting there
　I saw the lightened streaks
　　　of sun lay down
　　upon the paling rock
　　　and lay myself upon it too
those desert creatures each
　　　so still then watched them move

The Plant

Rubber around my foot
around my foot a sock
around my sock a pile of dirt
is getting wet a pile of mud
around my mind a thought
the foot means I am like a person to a thought
and the thought means I am like a plant to the sun

The earth feels made to the sky, no?

Fall asleep and dream you are a droplet
of pretty natural sugars condensed and spherical
then go get hid in someone's mouth like a candy
(maybe the groove in a tongue would be a nice place
    to stay)
and when they open their mouth for a raindrop
  you'll get a raindrop too

Yeah, well
my heart's a bean
wind clanking
windows
and in the air
again I hear
thin happy music
about being alone

strands of gold
a powdered clover
in my box

the shallot-colored
beaks of birds
peck at my legs

the sun
and the little peach
float around each other
all day

Being of lambkin mind
and singular thought,
    I bleated out some thing
about the flower
    before I ate it.

        Green and yellow
    are two colors
        found in my field,
    I looked around
        and thought proudly.

On tracks I bake
in fields I lie down
bombs make holes
in buildings
and I go through
those holes like light
   I saw
     an old man living
in a quarry, and I saw
an old man living in a tank
I read about caves
and I read about
the first pretty flowers
in a glass dish growing
like a droplet or a pollywog
I split like an amoeba
into shy and passive tribes
which would I thought
fight and be done
   I saw a beaver from the window

awkward on land and thought
of that place covered in water
    now because of rain
this poem which was to be called
                Waste & Use
    will be called Image of Solace
Attempted in Your Name
                My little Ruby
        swims around
        in the mucky puddle
that was a yard
    and baby dogs
        have soft soft paws

Being in ways insatiable
lest thy planted flowers grow
get bigger and little blooming circles
come out of flowers
it's out of me here
as out of each living thing.
You cut a scallion and there's
a little green circle
it's like a field the smell the grass makes.
You cut a piece of straw, it's gold.
 sky's hatchet swiped at a tree
Rust's copper, its pretty color, cut it in half
and it's like sand again in the light.
Stupid world made up of fossils and moons.
We make people there and up they grow.
You don't cut them in half.
Ice, which is water in its solid form,
is grey and the world too from far away,
people telling stories of what happened,
a whole wood post stuck in the dirt

and a butterfly
with two matching and colorful wings
landed there and the little boy
grabbed at it and got his hand stuck
with peckings of splinter then
that butterfly above his head
flapping like a wondered idea.

confident
I had forgotten everything
and useless (sic)
        I wandered with Anthony
    through the desert
        looking at white
            dried out shrubs
        and crushing tinny rocks with feet

        light brown desert
        full of bushes and light

clappers clapping happy of here
and sound is what the world
has made of itself
being loud and also playing

a way a call things booming
out into the sky as
an open mouth blows
a bubble of what it says

Hazy warm presence of us too
being ourselves (each as a been thing)
our bodies devised it and then
made it what it said

O

and together

moon
lights
out
windows
and seas
large dark scale
on beach
like reeds
we sway and pulse
expectantly
at night
the things we do
we see

reveling in the
  light
        not of a
thing, just left
the door open
like it was summer

        and walked out

                                    rain

                    summer showers

         rubbing soap

         on all myself

                    and having nosey

                                    summer thoughts

                    of Oregon

                                    storm

                    flowers dipping

         out of herbs

         their purple mouths

light sand
  which blows up
    with air
beneath it a cloth
      spreads itself out
      but what sort of self
        does it have

I felt sad feeling
knowing and knowing
but that's me

  knelt down
  bowed down
and then over you
and then under you
    like a plant
    which can't move
but always shines

its yellow face
for the sun

and sways

shell plucked
from the stony shore
and kept around
for this big house to enclose

a plaster bath
a room and shutter
the windows a wind

my bedroom quiet
warm and clean

flap flap
go the
dying
yellow leaves

*

starlings described
for the people I see
    their heads poke out
looking to feed, and
    they're singing
and they're occupying trees

flower puffs of dust
in city's falling sky
wind down street
and birds on wind
I say leaf's flood of loving people
I'm among
but less a body
less a body's mind

junk plums gathered
by their spirit
for I thought
is what I thought
when I stopped outside
the building
city pups
slack and drugged
I feel my body tense
my bowels the lower part
of my back
the breeze
soft tapping
is the cicada
like a rim around me closing
and tears,
I think

Powder's
glowing sandals
get me round
while I, inside
some sad thing
saw you in your yard
poking around
those weed flowers
saying, my soul and
the parts of myself
me too
my arrogant take
on places and things
a fire
consumed my body
and everyone
tells you to quit

Raise while you can
little planks of ice
lotuslike shape of lake, slab
and receding tangible bank in storm.

See how now our nose is pointed down
with the powdered effect of an unreal cloud

I drew a little line
so the deer could cross
with beautiful pirouettes and balletish muscles
they went by

On certain days the lake feels like
a pair of fingers
clasped down on a metal notch
with soft white gloves

I'm embarrassed about it now
but my face was the same face
with a big bush island for an eye

47

Graceful and swift are the animals
    in the pouring and heavy fog
    and in the sun alike

Potatoes crushed in earth
rot in various concoctions

I draw a line with my finger through the field
    that water might naturally be inclined
        to follow it down and it does

Here I have convoluted two natural things:

A family of antelope
turned to look at me

and a froze lake
beside which I have waited,
my life to proceed.

Daisies are calming
like horns in some unison of exuberance
 I once made out in the warm air
and like a pedal pedal of
the whole world gently serenaded
I stood there

    See my feet
              in the dirt
                 with the plants

did I say bees which flew or tears of water, no.
Fish's little lips breaking the surface
        for what?
                    For a fly.
White fly living out all its charming hours
and then nothing
             down, out, on the river's water to float
  you into me

or me into you
      says the fish, goodness
I'm just pleased we ended up here together.

That's Not What I'd Do

Aquariums radiant with fishes
and haberdasheries stoned as rocks were dumb
        sitting there—cries repeated
    outraged, cavernous, dapper & smarty, here's
my little dressed-up poem, it's
got a hat it's got these fancy shoes it feels
like everyone's watching it when everyone's not.
The blue ghosts of what they call equipage
    float around it like patient dissatisfied lovers,
and people who don't know still stare at it
their silhouettes reptilian and mod
                shadows of actual things caught falling
    upon them.
Did you ever notice how leaves when speaking of
    where they're from glare and pout?
I am alone, so feeling the way I do
    I fall upon those about me and even
    as they run, there I am
        dry dry and falling, mwah.

On 13th street
where there are cherry trees
and children brought
by their parents to live
in calm patterned seclusions kept
the day flowers and in a bowl
I poured the water.

If one feels nothing
and still sees, sees with his eyes
if one sees with his eyes sees with his eyes

Early end of year
            smelled smoke
and little lifts of cooler air

    I looked into the darken woods
    and thought it's day

        I'm thinking now
        of what light's left
        there in the trees

Baby snows come in October
    I see them
in my mind
       they're crystalline
and eachy

      you
   are likely staying
     warm and seeing
     through windows
   or no,
 you've gone out
    into it already,
  purposeless
 <u>first snow</u>
    and I was heading
home expecting apples

on a twig in its frame
lives my yellow bird
and when I get drunk
it flies around

Crackle crackle
 little hails on my hat
clicking their notes atone
   hear this: an awning to
      bounce off of, and the things
you saved up
   for dreams came down speaking.

No strange light
as lead making little marks
on the field on the tree
where wasps the smoky bluish air.
I am not encumbered by those things
which the flattened embanking leaves
beneath your spread coat portend.
I'm going to call this poem windows,
win-dows win-dows
repeat as strange song in head
until bus comes.
The red light wire
which is like a needle
thread through the ear of a sleeping girl
or boy, I can never tell,
hung there thinly dazzling.
I'm gonna call this poem porch light,
porch light porch light.
Over the hillside with magnificent ritual

they strode, their eyes
scanning the treetops to see
a branch right for a funeral box,
a grass hinge in the fire fluttering.

<u>Sitting on that chair</u>
<u>a peg above my head</u>

Toward the beach
the waves were crashing
and periodically a drop
of water would be thrown
into the air

and land on a stem
of beach grass

  this happened in the morning
and in the night, it happened
at times the moon was shining
it was and at times
a burning white gray sky
that is also water

one lost arrow
stretched out in a line

toooo toooo
cried the ghost
of the little girl who was dead
now attacked by sun
and so called out

                    wooden slatted bridge
                    as into town

and the ground took parts
of a bottle back

Pan's crowd were
musicians too
    sleeping at night
  like white shells
    reflecting moon
<u>earth stars</u>
    kids call them
  pick them up
put them in their pockets

Park hurt calls
yelling and looking
for a first unangry place to land,
    roots in the ground
   and the snow came down
        on the tree. You'll
          grow later I thought
       for the sun.

            It was
    the splendid story of the caterpillar
that inspired both the row house and
the airechute. Its fast spectacular ending life
and the way it's made up of all those parts.

"Do you hope for mastery of yourself
or of the other living things
or of the other unliving things,
I think you must decide."

        Now?
            I asked.

and that's the story of
the butterfly, which as I said before
inspired the ice pond and the worker's break,
then flew away so colorfully
never to return.

How the mountain
calmed me down

bone
stick
pebble
little
hot sun burnt
in grass
and now
you
there
getting ready
to leave
and me
(it's my body)
can't hear a thing
later then
looking at sticks
I breathe

Not gloss year candles
in the shining light already
    but it was fall
the rains had come
        and soaking leaves
    did soak the darkened street
            no moon
                because of
    clouds and storm
        my home so
full of air this summer
        now was big was cold

Ocean which I pushed up
with my fingers so I could touch
the orange sand below

and white mountain
which is not white but for getting
caught in the cold

Stay here where it is warm
and where the sun shines, for later
celestial garlands of dead light
will draw you into the cold for sure

<u>full of scarlet</u> as birds
are on their forelocks
flicking golden caviars of dead fish
into the air,

                no sated life
  of turned plaster bust
how it

          resembles a piece of wood
eaten down by a body of water
while still alive in moony sphere
like a cut-out circle of paper circles
in human time the sky

             it's animals really
their pumping hearts it makes their bodies
full with blood and their skin
with all those feeling nerves
I felt that too,

             your hand on a cold apple's
  bruised face, the blood running through
    and we're making out

God's cabin's a jungle
ain't no fear of lions there.
Green greenery shootin like arrows
from the ground
and plant oils rollin down
also rain
if you rot you're a log
if you run you're a river,
otherwise just spiderwebs and
falling asleep spiders
and there's a drip too
sometimes no light
sometimes light like the moon
sometimes light like a crack comes through itself
sorry to be one of two things
but not sorry to be that one.
I placed my foot down on a moss
which I made die
and then my knee the same.
Sometimes I see what is seen of me.

The wet black bark of the forest
did cough and shake unknowingly
and the time that hail came down cold and
hard upon it, let us shiver
that things may feel and feelings go
and that high loud call of timber
stretched upon itself will break
then breaking done will stand up straight.

*

Smiling granite
    cliffs and church
  of pewter stars
     first carried strange
then dropped in yard
    its bolded stone
   and hailing too
   and hailing too
and getting dark

Couldn't then see
in dark unpersonal things
a stream of brass
   flashing through
like sunlit spot
on shaded stream
or streak in
   fish's leather coat
but it's people
   the vibrant
calcium in their bones

Not as in some
    curled fascination
like the sun does
    with its discus
    (magnificent piercing
        cries collected,
    waiting, deadish as
        a man, his stare
    beneath the lonesome
    rust-covered wood)
but in clouds
    which were not there
and are there now
                raining water
            onto the earth
        where beauty is found
        in things at times

The burdened cry
or <u>madrigal of</u>
<u>trashbird</u> as beak is
when jabbed into
grapefruit, seeds
knocking around
    the dusty sidewalk
  a strand
of human hair
    wrapped inexplicably
  around its beak
and as it hopped about
a little skill
did fill it
that it could lift things
that it could search still,
but feed and fix
it could not do
  so while its time
as might be clear

ran short too soon
  it cast briefly
    a rough and bold figure
lifting itself from the weeds

     one sun up
      one sun down

the darkness there
in watered mist

alive
a little pointed hand

It's not a funny thing
watching a star land in a boy's mouth
or a big moon shine down
on a dead hill
or the showy light from a sun
spread out on a cold self
God's Wicker Basket Furnace
is like a nickname we gave our state
drunk as we were, but still
full of love, the milky way
the many stars their stupid
ancient stories click.

stars which
   started separate
split and fall
in form of mind
 the way I mean beings
    made of themselves
fantastic domes
  and structures make math
   (is that right?)
      living also mouth
of the north
     I threw
myself onto the couch
   (cassiopeia)
which in ancient times
was like drawing a dot of light
through some overcasting fabric
that flapped about beside the sun
  The Curtain
is what I'd call our constellation

growinggrowing
fill of sky
and then snow and then fire
from the lamp poles froze
the sight of which made us warm
love's globey too
turning above it
a pantomime of showy night
like the field
where sky's spirit
got powdered 2 to zip

living real things
and stupid coming out with my now
now love's question
cracks and sounds
as I watch you
that's where you are
a big white picture
of a glacier
in your office

a bit of
   combed hair
 combed

            you
   came in from the
 cold outside
  a sad sort of
      fold in your eye
 parts
     of thoughts
    on tongues
  to former lovers come.

                    tablets
        made from dead grey
water,
                    winter
        reeds
            colder
                later froze
        kinda froze
            with a boat
                    left in it

I saw hearts in Proust
making pillows out of people's
thoughts and clever puffy clouds
elegant in their certitude
getting blown westward
and when I made my bed
with those clean white sheets
and slipped into it my body
I felt as if the whole sleeping world
had come to make me quiet too.
I picked up a book and put it down.

a hammer flattens
a flat tin plaque

a dead tree
shakes

and brick
and glass
and wood
and smoke

Grey light shadow
and big attic bulb
(for Vic)
ever out
at night
a kind of
glass

           caution's loving
sentiment
                is

                    time

and fearful slow
I pulse out words

and hear the words
that others speak

                    I struggle too
        to say it now

        my body's
        living cold
        but no one saw

and man made coats

falling terrors of
feeling night
   so gotten down
  this storied tumbling
roar of wind
   and batted brush
 I write
   of canyon rocks
  and point out pretty
    colored shapes
then cower in my shaking room

hot in my frame
this human way
to feel around
  on my shoulders
  on my face

Lofted cold falls
        splash weak
in symphony
    of earth still on
a bird under
        an outward rock
and pooled as pooled
    in cloud above
        the shallow swells

        Later that year
a baby and later still
    the massive rock
        formation in the
        picture disappeared

Let my still dark soul
be music. A made whistle
floating out a window
arranged.

Some little thing
fell and I picked it up
and up it kept on going.

Eight dead stars
make a sickle,
and the earth
is covered in grass.